Battles of the American Revolution Saratoga

VICTORIA RUSHWORTH

Table of Contents

Pictures To Think About

Battles of the American Revolution: Saratoga

THE BATTLE OF SARATOGA
September 19, 1777

Burgoyne

Fraser

Hamilton and
Burgoyne

Freeman's Farm

NEW YORK

Mill Creek

Riedesel

BEMIS HEIGHTS

Arnold
and
Morgan

Learned

Gates

Hudson River

Bemis's
Tavern

SCALE OF MILES
0   1/2   1

British troops
American troops

Words To Think About

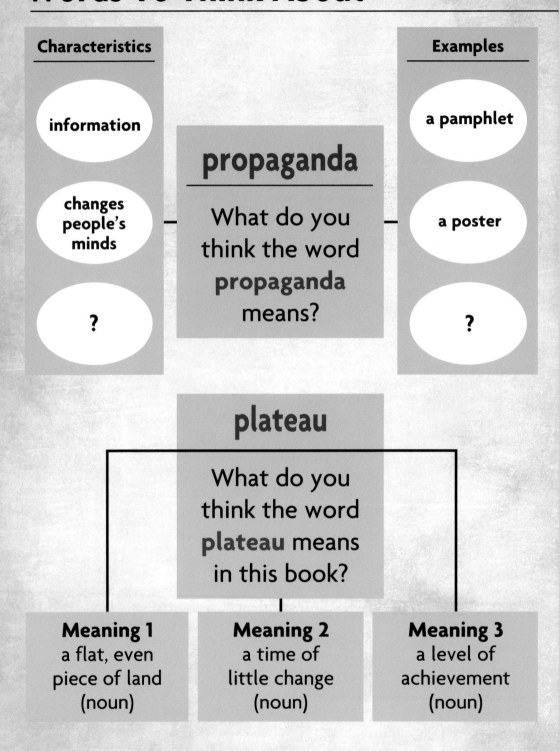

Characteristics

information

changes people's minds

?

propaganda

What do you think the word **propaganda** means?

Examples

a pamphlet

a poster

?

plateau

What do you think the word **plateau** means in this book?

Meaning 1
a flat, even piece of land (noun)

Meaning 2
a time of little change (noun)

Meaning 3
a level of achievement (noun)

Read for More Clues
militia,   page 9
plateau,   page 19
propaganda, page 16

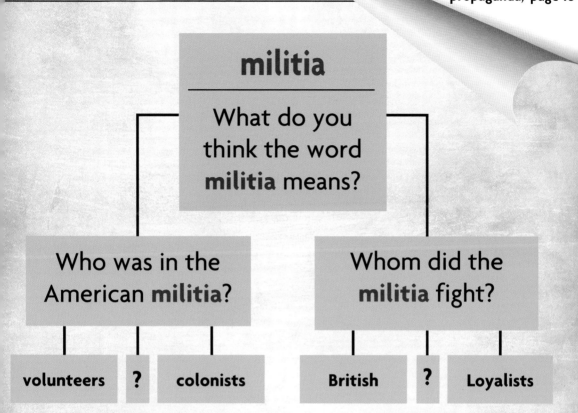

militia

What do you think the word **militia** means?

Who was in the American **militia**?

volunteers   **?**   colonists

Whom did the **militia** fight?

British   **?**   Loyalists

Introduction

Every war is a series of battles. Wars are won on the battlefield. The strongest army does not always win every battle.

Sometimes the weather or landscape affects the outcome of the battle. Other times, leaders make choices that affect who wins or loses. All of these factors played a role in the battles of the Revolutionary War.

During this war, the battles did not happen in a distant land. The American and British troops fought in the fields of America.

The Battles of Saratoga took place in a clearing in the woods. The battles took place in the Fall of 1777. The first battle was on September 19, 1777. The second battle began on October 7th.

▼ Saratoga National Historical Park, NY

THE BATTLES OF SARATOGA

Dates: September 19th, 1777–October 17th, 1777
Locations: Freeman's Farm, outside Saratoga, New York
     Bemis Heights, outside Saratoga, New York
Weather: Mild, cloudy, rainy

American Leaders:
General Horatio Gates
General Benedict Arnold
Colonel Daniel Morgan

British Leaders:
General John Burgoyne
Baron Friedrich Riedesel
General Simon Fraser

American Casualties:
800 killed, wounded, and missing

British Casualties:
1,600 killed, wounded, and missing
6,000 surrendered

The battles of Saratoga were very important. These battles changed how the war would end. These battles showed the world that the Americans could win the war.

Before Saratoga, France gave guns to the Americans. When America won at Saratoga, France gave full support to the American cause. France would now supply men, money, as well as guns. This would help the Americans win the war.

In this book, you will go behind the scenes at Saratoga. You will meet the people who played a part in these battles. You will also learn about the factors that played a part in these battles.

Read on to learn how these battles changed history.

The Stage Is Set

In December 1777, John Burgoyne (ber-GOYN) had an idea. Burgoyne thought he knew how to end the war. His plan was to cut the rebel army in half. He would surround the rebel forces in the North. Then the New England states would be cut off from the rest of the country.

Burgoyne would divide his army into three columns, or groups. Burgoyne would lead the main column south from Canada. He and his men would travel down the Hudson River.

General William Howe would lead the second column. Howe would march his army north from New York City. The two columns would meet in Albany, New York.

Meanwhile, a third column would travel from Canada down the Mohawk River. Colonel Barry St. Leger (SAYNT LEH-jer) would lead that column. Burgoyne thought this plan would win the war.

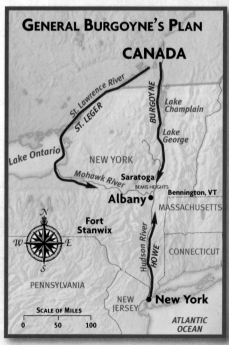

▲ Burgoyne divided his army into three columns.

LEADERS OF THE FIGHT

General John Burgoyne was born in London on February 24, 1722. When he was fifteen, he joined the army. Burgoyne earned a reputation as a gambler. He also loved the theater and liked to write. One of his plays was produced on the London stage.

At the age of twenty-eight, he married the daughter of an earl. Her family did not approve. Her father would not give them any money. Burgoyne's salary could barely cover his gambling debts. So he sold his commission to raise money. In those days, officers had to buy a commission in the army. Later, Burgoyne was able to buy himself a place in the army again. Burgoyne was sent to Boston, Massachusetts, to fight the American rebels. He was there for the Battle of Bunker Hill. Afterward, he returned to England.

In 1777, King George III agreed to send Burgoyne back to Canada with close to 7,000 troops to fight in the Revolution. After his defeat at Saratoga, Burgoyne went home to London. He lived the rest of his life quietly. He started writing again and even wrote a successful play. Burgoyne died in London on June 4, 1792.

SOLDIERS OF THE WAR

The German soldiers who fought in the American Revolution were known as "**Hessians.**" The soldiers were hired by the British, who simply did not have enough soldiers of their own. British regulars were on duty in Ireland, the West Indies, and other countries in the British Empire. Some 20,000 German soldiers served in the American Revolution. The first German king to offer troops was Friedrich II of Hesse-Cassel. That is where the term "Hessian" comes from. The official name of the soldiers was **Brunswickers** (BRUNZ-wik-ers).

▲ Hessian soldiers

Burgoyne had made one big mistake. He did not think about the land in the region. The **terrain** (tuh-RANE) was rough. The land had many mountains and thick forests.

Most of the region was still not settled. The towns were far apart. The British did not know how big America was.

None of this worried Burgoyne. He set sail for Canada with 7,000 troops.

A Good Beginning

Burgoyne set off from Canada in June of 1777. He had about 9,000 men with him. Among them were British soldiers, German soldiers, Canadian soldiers, and Native Americans. The Native Americans were scouts. Scouts guided the troops through the wilderness.

The journey to Albany was not easy. The men had to cut roads through the forest. They had to build bridges across rivers.

The American rebels made the trip even more difficult. The rebels left nothing in their trail. They burned crops and houses. They took along livestock or set them free. They cut down trees to block the roads. They also tore down bridges.

WOMEN OF THE WAR

Many of the ships that crossed the Atlantic with Burgoyne included women. It was not unusual for women to travel with the troops. Each army had women to cook for them and do laundry. Wives of both regular soldiers and officers followed their men into battle. One such woman was Lady Harriet Acland. She was the wife of a major who fought at Saratoga. Her husband was wounded and taken prisoner by the Americans. Even though she was pregnant, Lady Harriet crossed the river to the enemy camp at night. She asked permission to nurse her husband. American general Horatio Gates allowed her to do so.

A TURN OF EVENTS

The British attacked Fort Stanwix. They hoped the **siege** (SEEJ) would force the Americans to give up. Instead, the American general Benedict Arnold forced the British out.

Burgoyne learned about the setback at Fort Stanwix. It was bad news. He also had heard nothing from General Howe.

Howe's troops should have been marching north from New York City.

Supplies were running low. Burgoyne decided to send his men into Vermont. His men would get fresh supplies and more horses there. He did not know that there were rebel soldiers in Vermont.

They Made a Difference

▲ Colonel Barry St. Leger

Benedict Arnold convinced the British to give up Fort Stanwix through a trick. He made a deal with an American man named Hon Yost. Yost was a **Loyalist**, who had been captured by the Americans. Yost had to convince the Indians fighting with the British that a huge rebel force was marching toward them. If he did, he could go free. Yost did a good job. The Indians believed him and took off into the forest. Without the Indians to help him fight, St. Leger retreated. It was all a trick. There never was a huge army of rebels.

"*The moment is a decisive one.*"
–*General Burgoyne on his decision to march to Albany at all costs*

In Vermont, Burgoyne's troops were attacked by American **militia** (mih-LIH-shuh) units. These were units of volunteer soldiers. More than 200 of Burgoyne's men died. Seven hundred of Burgoyne's men were captured.

Only forty Americans were killed. Just thirty were wounded. Burgoyne did not get his supplies. Still, he did not give up.

Solve This

General Burgoyne's 9,000 men had enough food to last thirty days. Each man consumed one half pound of food per day. How many pounds of food were required to feed the men for thirty days?

Historical Perspective

In colonial wartime, food was a big concern. Food did not stay fresh very long. It was hard to find more. Soldiers carried flour to make their own bread. Today's armies carry food that has been canned or freeze-dried. It can last for months.

They Made a Difference

The troops that fought in the Revolution were from state militias and the Continental army. The militias had existed in the colonies since before the war. When they were needed, those men would defend their own territory. They usually signed up for a short time and then returned home. All during the war this was a problem for the officers in charge.

No matter where he was, even in the middle of battle, when a man's time was up, he could simply leave. On the one hand, this made sense. Most of the men in the militias were farmers. They were needed at home to grow food. No food at home meant no food for the troops.

▲ Continental army soldier

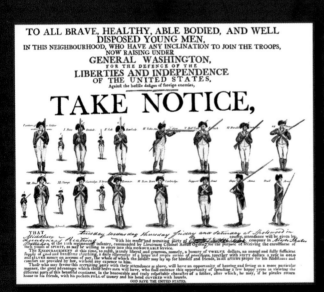

The Continental army was created by Congress after the Battle of Bunker Hill. It was commanded by George Washington. Most of the time, men enlisted for a year or two. Many deserted because Congress could not pay them or feed them.

Moving On

General Burgoyne had to make a choice. There were two ways to get to Albany. Both ways were dangerous.

One way was along the east bank of the Hudson River. There would not be many rebel troops on the east side of the river.

The British would have to cross the river where it was wide and deep. American troops and their cannons would be in the hills above the river. The British would then have to climb the steep banks along the river. The British would be easy targets.

The other way was to cross the Hudson first. Then the men would go down the west side of the river. The crossing would be easier. But there were many rebel troops on the west side of the river. The British would have to fight

the rebels all the way to Albany. Albany was forty-five miles (72 kilometers) away.

▲ Burgoyne's march to Albany

2 Solve This

Each wagon Burgoyne had with him could hold 2,500 pounds of food. How many wagons did General Burgoyne need to transport one month's worth of rations? (Use the answer from the first Solve This on page 9.)

11

British Uniforms

1768 clothing warrant
–Regulations for the
Clothing of Marching
Regiments of the Foot

CAPS FOR GRENADIER OFFICERS
The Officers of the grenadiers wore black bear-skin caps.

HATS
The hats were laced either with gold or silver.

EPAULETTES
The Officers of **grenadiers** wore an epaulette on each shoulder. They were either of embroidery or lace, with gold or silver fringe.

UNIFORM OF OFFICERS
The number of each regiment was on the buttons of the uniforms of the Officers and men.

WAISTCOATS
The waistcoats were plain, without either embroidery or lace.

SWORDS
The swords of each regiment were uniform. The hilts were either gilt or silver, according to the color of the buttons on the uniforms.

CARTRIDGE BOX
Each side of the box held 18 rounds of ammunition.

American Uniforms
Second Massachusetts Regiment of Continental Infantry, 1777

Unlike the British, the American soldiers were not all dressed alike. For one thing, the soldiers came from different militias. And there was little money for fancy uniforms.

Before 1779, there was no regulation uniform for the Massachusetts regiments in Continental service. But most Massachusetts soldiers who had uniforms wore blue coats faced and lined with white.

The regiments were recognized by the numbers stamped on the pewter buttons.

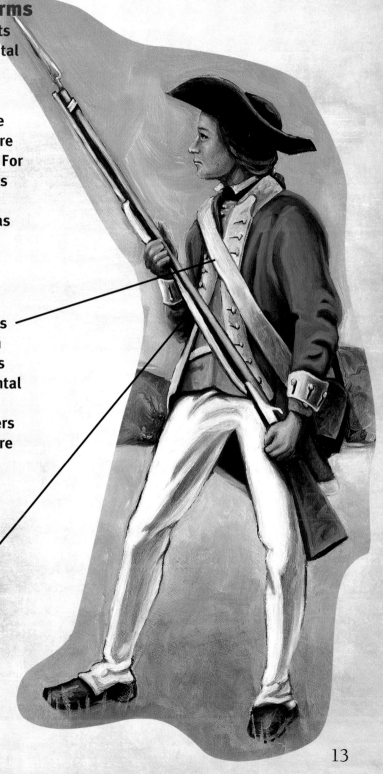

A CHOICE IS MADE

Burgoyne made a choice. His army would cross the river first. Then they would march down the west side.

The British had four week's **provisions** (pruh-VIH-zhunz). This meant they had enough supplies to last four weeks. They had to reach Albany in one month. If not, they might starve.

September 13, 1777, was a bright, sunny day. The troops marched across a bridge made of boats tied together. Two days later, General Riedesel and the German soldiers followed.

3 Solve This

Each one of General Burgoyne's wagons was drawn by two horses. How many horses were required to pull all the wagons? (Use the answer from the second Solve This on page 11.)

THEY MADE A DIFFERENCE

Friedrich Adolph Riedesel was in charge of the German soldiers who fought alongside General Burgoyne.

He was born in 1738 into a German noble family. He left home at age fifteen to study. At school, he loved to watch the Hesse troops drill. When he was seventeen, a friend told Riedesel his father had given him permission to become a soldier. But it was a lie.

When the Duke of Brunswick agreed to "rent" soldiers to the British during the Revolutionary War, it was Major General Riedesel who was put in charge. Riedesel and his family arrived in Canada in June of 1777.

After the war, Riedesel returned to Germany. He arrived home with less than half of the soldiers that he had set out with. Riedesel died at home on January 6, 1800.

When all the men had crossed, the boats were untied. The British troops could no longer go back to Canada.

The soldiers marched in three columns. The **artillery**, or the guns and ammunition, were in the middle. On the right were the British troops. On the left were the Germans. There were 6,500 soldiers in all.

The army that set off that morning was hungry and tired. They knew the rebels would be waiting for them along the way.

It's a Fact

The army was not alone. Burgoyne's troops were joined by hundreds of camp followers. These included members of the clergy, doctors, women, and children. Officers had servants. General Riedesel's wife even had her own carriage.

▲ **Baroness Riedesel and family**

15

THE AMERICANS PREPARE

General Burgoyne reached Saratoga and began his **campaign** (kam-PANE).

Meanwhile, American troops were camped to the south. Major General Horatio Gates was in charge. His men were getting ready to fight.

Primary Source

". . . an aide-de-camp showed me a fresh scalp-lock which I could not mistake."
—Jane McCrae's fiancé

WOMEN OF THE WAR

The murder of an American woman was used as **propaganda** (prah-puh-GAN-duh) to excite rebels against the British. Jane McCrae lived in Saratoga with one of her brothers. At the start of the war, two of her brothers joined the American forces. But the man she was to marry was a Loyalist. He went to Canada to join the British. He became a soldier in Burgoyne's army. Jane was on her way to meet him when she and another woman were captured by a band of Indians who were fighting with the British.

▲ Jane McCrae

There are different stories about what happened next. But one way or another, Jane was murdered by her captors and scalped. The scalps were taken to Burgoyne's camp. There, McCrae's fiancé recognized her hair. McCrae is buried near Fort Edward in New York. In 2003, her body was exhumed. Experts hoped to learn more about her death, but they did not.

SOLDIERS OF THE WAR

Horatio Gates was born in England in 1728. His parents were servants. As a young man, he joined the British army. He fought in the French and Indian Wars in America. Gates resigned from the British Army in 1772. He retired to live in Virginia. But his military career was only beginning. He soon became involved in the rebel cause. As soon as the Revolution started, Gates joined up. His first major command was to head up the Northern department of the war. He took over on August 19th, just in time for Saratoga.

Gates is famous for his victory over Burgoyne. But he was never on the battlefield. In fact, he never left his headquarters.

After Saratoga, Gates continued to serve. But he was never again a winning commander. In fact, he was accused of leaving the scene of battle and was investigated. Nothing came of it. Gates retired from army life in 1784. He moved to New York where he died in 1806.

General Horatio Gates ▶

Gates had close to 10,000 soldiers. One of the most important was Daniel Morgan.

Morgan led the Virginia riflemen. His men were expert shots and fine scouts. They could creep through the woods as quietly as any Native American scout.

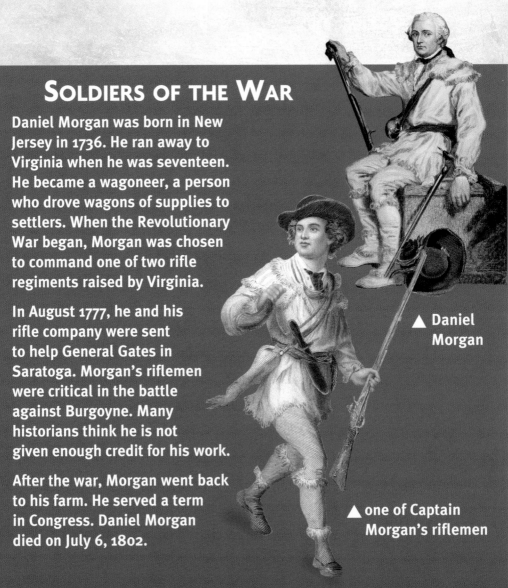

SOLDIERS OF THE WAR

Daniel Morgan was born in New Jersey in 1736. He ran away to Virginia when he was seventeen. He became a wagoneer, a person who drove wagons of supplies to settlers. When the Revolutionary War began, Morgan was chosen to command one of two rifle regiments raised by Virginia.

In August 1777, he and his rifle company were sent to help General Gates in Saratoga. Morgan's riflemen were critical in the battle against Burgoyne. Many historians think he is not given enough credit for his work.

After the war, Morgan went back to his farm. He served a term in Congress. Daniel Morgan died on July 6, 1802.

▲ Daniel Morgan

▲ one of Captain Morgan's riflemen

Gates's troops were camped about halfway between Albany and Saratoga. The scouts went out to find a place to meet the enemy. Local people told them about Bemis Heights.

Bemis Heights was a **plateau** (pla-TOH), or flat piece of land. The plateau had many trees. It was higher than the land around it. From the top of the hill, a soldier could see for miles in every direction.

The men cleared a passage below the hill. The passage was narrow. The only road to Albany ran through the passage. Burgoyne's troops would soon come marching down that road. They would be easy targets.

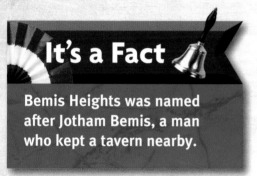

It's a Fact

Bemis Heights was named after Jotham Bemis, a man who kept a tavern nearby.

▼ Bemis Heights

The Battles

General Burgoyne had seen the rebels at Bemis Heights. Burgoyne did not know what Gates had planned. General Burgoyne knew the only road to Albany would go right past Bemis Heights.

General Gates sent Daniel Morgan and his men to spy on Burgoyne's army. Gates knew Burgoyne had to move soon. Both sides knew a battle was only days away.

SEPTEMBER 19: BATTLE DAY

The early morning of Friday, September 19, was foggy and cold. The thick fog made it hard to see. American scouts saw movement in the British camp.

▲ British soldiers

 **POINT**

Picture It

Reread pages 20–21. Imagine you are an American scout. What would you have seen when the fog cleared?

The British began to move out. The British broke into three columns. One column moved far out to the right. This column was led by General Simon Fraser.

The left column was led by General Riedesel. It marched along the river. It held all the heavy artillery, light and heavy cannons, and guns. Each of the columns had about 2,500 men.

The main army marched down the middle. General Burgoyne and his staff rode with the main force of 1,700 men.

Gates was willing to wait and see what Burgoyne did. General Benedict Arnold did not want to wait.

Arnold was always quick to act. He told Morgan and his men to march to the woods. Morgan and his men climbed trees to wait for the enemy.

THE BATTLE OF SARATOGA
September 19, 1777

Burgoyne

Hamilton and Burgoyne
Fraser
Freeman's Farm

NEW YORK

Mill Creek

Riedesel

BEMIS HEIGHTS

Arnold and Morgan
Learned
Gates

Hudson River

N
W E
S

Bemis's Tavern

SCALE OF MILES
0   1/2

British troops
American troops

▲ **Benedict Arnold**

21

"Both armies seemed determined to conquer or die."
–General Clover

SHOTS ARE FIRED

At about one in the afternoon, 300 British soldiers came over a hill. These soldiers entered a clearing known as Freeman's Farm. Morgan's riflemen saw the soldiers and fired. Almost at once, the front line dropped to the ground.

The riflemen were so excited at their success that they ran out from the cover of the trees. It was a fatal mistake. General Fraser's men arrived and fired. The riflemen were hit.

Gates ordered more soldiers to the field to help Morgan's men. Now rebels and British were face to face on the field of battle.

Primary Source

One American soldier described the guns firing without stop. He called it, "the hottest fire of cannon . . . that I ever heard in my life."

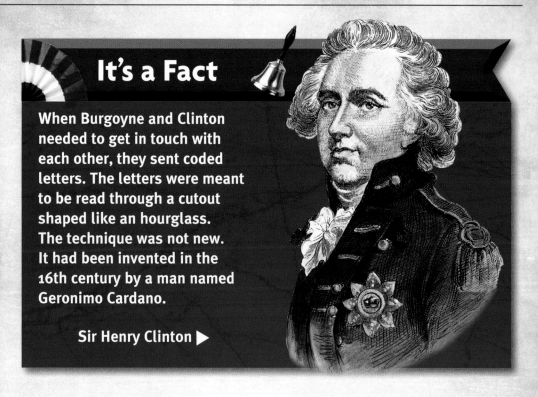

It's a Fact

When Burgoyne and Clinton needed to get in touch with each other, they sent coded letters. The letters were meant to be read through a cutout shaped like an hourglass. The technique was not new. It had been invented in the 16th century by a man named Geronimo Cardano.

Sir Henry Clinton ▶

The fighting raged on for hours. First one side seemed to be winning. Then the other side seemed to be ahead. Soon the dead and dying were everywhere.

At last it got dark. The Americans fell back. The British had won the day. Still, Burgoyne had lost 160 men. Another 364 were wounded and 42 were missing. The Americans had lost about 300 men, but new troops came to replace them.

A LETTER OF FALSE HOPE

On September 21, Burgoyne got a letter. The letter was from Sir Henry Clinton. Clinton was the commander of British forces in New York City. Clinton said that he expected to arrive with more men in about ten days.

Burgoyne waited for Clinton's troops. Every day more men died. There were not enough blankets or tents. Many soldiers slept on the bare ground. Men were on constant guard duty.

General Gates was also waiting. He thought Burgoyne was running low on supplies and food. Gates himself was low on ammunition.

Nearly three weeks passed. Time was running out. Burgoyne had to press on. He could not wait for Clinton's troops. On October 4, Burgoyne met with his generals.

OCTOBER 7: ONE LAST STAND

Burgoyne wanted to attack again. He planned to leave 800 men on the river. They would guard the supplies and the hospital. The other 4,000 men would attack Gates.

Burgoyne's generals did not agree with him. Riedesel thought they should not risk all the men on just one mission. Burgoyne gave in. Burgoyne agreed to send only 2,000 men.

General Horatio Gates ▶

THE BATTLE OF SARATOGA
October 7, 1777

Sword's Farm

Breymann's Redoubt

Great Redoubt

Freeman's Farm

Burgoyne's Headquarters

Arnold

British bridge of boats

NEW YORK

BEMIS HEIGHTS

Mill Creek

Hudson River

N
W · E
S

Gates's Headquarters

SCALE OF MILES
0   1/2   1

Bemis's Tavern

British troops
American troops

was made up of British and Germans. In the center was General Riedesel.

The Americans were ready. They attacked. General Fraser was badly wounded. The British tried to fall back. Benedict Arnold's troops would not let them.

At 1 p.m., the British soldiers were ready to march. Once again, Burgoyne divided the men into three columns. On the right was Fraser's column. The left column

25

Arnold had been ordered by Gates to stay away. Arnold didn't. He grabbed a horse and charged into the battle. He took command of the troops and attacked.

Arnold's courage won the day for the Americans. Again and again he rode across the battle lines. Arnold stopped only when he was shot in the leg.

The British began to retreat to Saratoga. Baroness Riedesel was among them. Her diary tells of their march.

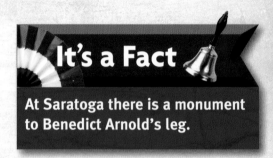

It's a Fact

At Saratoga there is a monument to Benedict Arnold's leg.

SOLDIERS OF THE WAR

Had Benedict Arnold died on the battlefield at Saratoga, he would be remembered today as a hero. But later in the war, he became a spy for the British. He planned to hand the keys to the fort at West Point to the British. But the plot was uncovered. Arnold managed to escape to England. He died there in 1801. His place in history is as a traitor, not a hero.

▲ Benedict Arnold

 ## Primary Source

Baroness Riedesel
The Defeat and Surrender of Burgoyne

"On the 9th, it rained terribly the whole day; nevertheless we kept ourselves ready to march. We reached Saratoga about dark . . . I was quite wet, and was obliged to remain in that condition, for want of a place to change my apparel. I seated myself near the fire, and undressed the children, and we then laid ourselves upon some straw. I refreshed myself at 7 o'clock, the next morning (the 10th of October), with a cup of tea. About 2 o'clock, we heard again a report of muskets and cannon . . . My husband sent me word, that I should immediately retire into a house which was not far off. Soon after our arrival, a terrible cannonade began, and . . . We were at last obliged to descend into the cellar . . . I laid myself in a corner near the door. My children put their heads upon my knees. An abominable smell, the cries of the children, and my own anguish of mind, did not permit me to close my eyes, during the whole night. On the next morning, the cannonade begun anew . . . Eleven cannon-balls passed through the house.

 ## POINT

Think About It
Reread page 27. What do you think the Baroness was thinking during the siege?

Conclusion

On October 17, at Saratoga, General Burgoyne surrendered to General Gates. The two men rode up to each other. They got off their horses. Burgoyne handed his sword to Gates. Gates held it for a moment. Then he gave the sword back to Burgoyne.

Next, the 6,000 British and German troops marched by the American troops. When they reached the riverbank, they put down their guns. The Americans stood by in complete silence.

▲ the surrender

THE TURNING POINT

The Battle of Saratoga changed the course of the American Revolution. The rebels had beaten the greatest military power in the world: Great Britain.

The win at Saratoga led both France and Spain to join the rebel cause. France and Spain helped the American rebels win the war. The end came when the British gave up at Yorktown in 1781. The American Revolution was over. America was a free country.

It's a Fact

As the British and German soldiers marched to surrender, they were trailed by the camp followers. Along with these men and women was a collection of deer, raccoons, and other wild animals who had become their pets.

4 Solve This

On average, members of the American militia were paid sixpence (about one nickel) per day. If the average term of enlistment was two months, (60 days) how much did a soldier earn?

Solve This Answers

Solve This 1 (Page 9)
135,000 pounds of food for thirty days

Solve This 2 (Page 11)
54 wagons

Solve This 3 (Page 14)
108 horses

Solve This 4 (Page 29)
60 days x .05 = $3.00 for two months' work

Glossary

artillery	(ar-TIH-ler-ee) heavy, cart-drawn guns and cannons (page 15)
Brunswicker	(BRUNZ-wik-er) another name for a Hessian or German soldier (page 6)
campaign	(kam-PANE) a series of military operations with a specific goal (page 16)
grenadier	(greh-nuh-DEER) a British soldier who threw grenades and made bombs (page 12)
Hessian	(HEH-shun) a German soldier who fought with the British in the American Revolution (page 6)
Loyalist	(LOY-uh-list) an American colonist who remained loyal to the king of England (page 8)
militia	(mih-LIH-shuh) an army of volunteer citizens organized during an emergency (page 9)
plateau	(pla-TOH) an elevated piece of land with a level surface (page 19)
propaganda	(prah-puh-GAN-duh) material designed to influence the opinion of a person or group (page 16)
provisions	(pruh-VIH-zhunz) the food and drink carried by a soldier (page 14)
siege	(SEEJ) constant and continuous battle over a specific place (page 8)
terrain	(tuh-RANE) another name for the type of land—wooded, or mountainous, for example—in an area (page 6)

Index